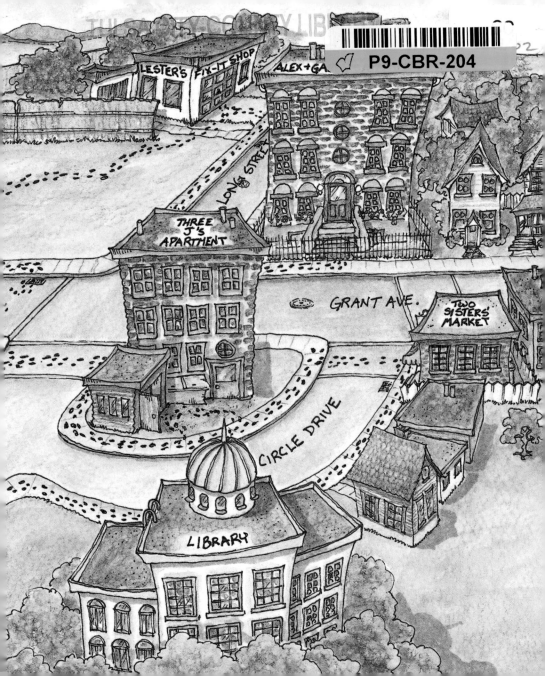

THE PROMISE

THE CORNER KIDS

Written by Larry Dane Brimner • Illustrated by Christine Tripp

Children's Press®
A Division of Scholastic Inc.
New York • Toronto • London • Auckland • Sydney
Mexico City • New Delhi • Hong Kong
Danbury, Connecticut

For Vicki Reed, storyteller par excellence
—L.D.B.

For my uncle, Don Snowdon, who gave me
my very first "technical pen" and my first
"professional" encouragement.
—C.T.

Reading Consultants
Linda Cornwell
Literacy Specialist

Katharine A. Kane
Education Consultant
(Retired, San Diego County Office of Education and San Diego State University)

Library of Congress Cataloging-in-Publication Data
Brimner, Larry Dane.
    The Promise/ written by Larry Dane Brimner; illustrated by Christine Tripp.
        p. cm.—(Rookie choices)
    Summary: Three J and Alex help Gabby keep a promise to her grandmother.
    ISBN: 0-516-22538-3 (lib. bdg.)   0-516-27388-4 (pbk.)
    [1. Promises—Fiction. 2. Friendship—Fiction. 3. Grandmothers—Fiction.] I. Tripp,
Christine, ill. II. Title. III. Series.
    PZ7.B767 Pr 2002
    [E]—dc21
                                                    2001003864

This book is about **friendship**.

Gabby was searching through the kitchen cupboard. "There," she said. She pulled out a plastic box and put it into her backpack.

Then she brushed her hands together as if the hard part were done. "All we need now is a frog."

"Right," said Three J.

Alex chuckled. "Remember last year?" he said. "Our frog didn't even move."

Gabby and Three J groaned. "Don't remind us," they said together.

7

Gabby, Three J, and Alex headed for the door. They called themselves the Corner Kids.

"Gabriela!" called Gabby's father. He peeked around the corner. "Aren't you forgetting something?"

Gabby turned around. "But the jumping contest is at lunchtime, and we still need a frog," she said.

11

"You did make a promise to your grandmother," Gabby's father reminded her.

Gabby sighed. "Abuela and I were going to plant some seeds over in the lot," she said to Three J and Alex. "She doesn't really need me."

13

Then she looked down.
"But I did make a promise."
She started back down the hall.

Three J and Alex started to leave.

Just outside the door Three J stopped. "Wait a minute!" he said.

Everyone looked at Three J.

17

"If we help, I bet there will still be time to find a frog and enter the contest," he said.

"You'd do that?" asked Gabby.

Three J shrugged.
"That's what friends are for."

In no time, the Corner Kids were helping Abuela rake the soil.

They were poking seeds into
the soft earth.

They were carrying pails
of sloshing water.

When the work was done, Abuela said, "Before you know it, this old lot will be a garden."

Everyone agreed.

27

Then Abuela checked her watch. "You know," she said, grinning, "there's a frog-jumping contest over at the library today. There's still time to enter if you hurry."

"Do you think?" said Gabby.
She hugged her grandmother
and then grabbed her backpack.
The Corner Kids shot down
the sidewalk.

"Find a jumper!" Abuela called after them.

That's just what the Corner Kids planned to do.

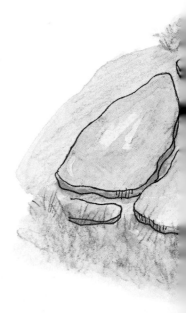

ABOUT THE AUTHOR

Larry Dane Brimner studied literature and writing at San Diego State University and taught school for twenty years. The author of more than seventy-five books for children, many of them Children's Press titles, he enjoys meeting young readers and writers when he isn't at his computer.

ABOUT THE ILLUSTRATOR

Christine Tripp lives in Ottawa, Canada, with her husband Don; four grown children—Elizabeth, Erin, Emily, and Eric; son-in-law Jason; grandsons Brandon and Kobe; four cats; and one very large, scruffy puppy named Jake.